AMBASSADORS OF HOPE

Sermons For Lent
And Easter
Cycle A, Second Lesson Texts

SANDRA HEFTER HERRMANN

CSS Publishing Company, Inc.
Lima, Ohio

AMBASSADORS OF HOPE

Scripture quotations are from the *New Revised Standard Version of the Bible,* copyright 1989, by the Division of Christian Education of the National Council of the Churches of Christ in the USA. Used by permission.

Library of Congress Cataloging-in-Publication Data

Herrmann, Sandra Hefter, 1944-
    Ambassadors of hope : sermons for Lent and Easter : Cycle A, second lesson texts / Sandra Hefter Herrmann.
        p.   cm.
    ISBN 0-7880-0478-6
    1. Lenten sermons. 2. Eastertide—Sermons. 3. Bible. N.T. Epistles—Sermons. 4. Sermons, English. 5. United Methodist Church (U.S.)—Sermons. 6. Methodist Church—Sermons. I. Title.
BV4277.H398   1995
252'.62—dc20   95-10577
                                                                                    CIP

This book is available in the following formats, listed by ISBN:
0-7880-0478-6 Book
0-7880-0479-4 IBM 3 1/2 computer disk
0-7880-0480-8 IBM 3 1/2 book and disk package
0-7880-0481-6 Macintosh computer disk
0-7880-0482-4 Macintosh book and disk package
0-7880-0483-2 IBM 5 1/4 computer disk
0-7880-0484-0 IBM 5 1/4 book and disk package

PRINTED IN U.S.A.

To Beth, who believed in me;
and to my mother:

> *"You may have wealth, and riches untold:*
> *caskets of jewels, silver and gold;*
> *but richer than I you never shall be:*
> *for I had a mother who read to me."*
> *— Author unknown*

Table Of Contents

Preface

This book was suggested to me by the former editor at CSS Publishing Company, Fred Steiner, for which I thank him. If it had not been for his encouragement and the specific assignment of the epistle lessons for the season, I would probably still be "considering" writing a book. A big thank you also goes to the present book editor, Terry Rhoads, who was coming on board and fielding my problems at the same time. Thank you both!

A second thank you needs to go to the members of my congregation at Faith United Methodist Church, Milwaukee, Wisconsin, for their indulgence and caring concern as I devoted the many hours it takes to work on such a project. Without your support, this project would not have been possible, either. Thank you, also, for listening as I "tried out" many of my ideas on you in sermons over the past year. You are a wonderful bunch of people!

Thank you, too, Beth — my friend and best fan — for doing so much to keep things running when the muse struck, and I was locked in the study typing furiously!

To all those friends who said I could do it, that I *did* have ideas worth putting on paper, who assured me that if I could preach it I could write it, thank you for supporting my fragile ego and sending me back to the computer again and again. And to George, Max and Snickerdoodle, who often had to come and tap my knee to get attention — I promise, hours of lap time for a month!

Halloween 1994

7

Introduction

When Fred Steiner talked to me about his idea for this book — a series of sermons on the epistle lessons for Lent through Easter — he told me this was a new idea, that he wasn't even sure the lessons would hang together, but wondered if I would look over the readings and let him know what I thought.

It took me two days to call him back and say, "This is a great idea! I'll do it." To me, the lessons hang together very well. They have a peculiar point of view: that we have been alienated from our true selves and our true country, deluded into thinking of God as oppressor or enemy. In order to win us back, God sent Jesus to negotiate for our release, to give himself as ransom so that we might be liberated. In turn, each of us is sent to bring word to those who are still in prison that they also are set free.

Many years ago, when I was working as a Christian Educator in the Black River Falls, Wisconsin, United Methodist Church, I was sent to Perkins School of Theology at Southern Methodist University for an upgrade program. There, I heard John Deschner talk about the centrality of the doctrine of the Trinity. He told us the story of a preacher who held up a filthy drinking glass, showing us, he said, how God sees us — filthy, unusable, fit only for destruction. Setting the glass down on a table, he raised a large hammer, thundering about God's intention to destroy sinful humans. As he brought down the hammer, he deftly picked up an aluminum pan, poised it between the hammer and the glass, and with a resounding clang, brought the hammer down on the pan. The problem with this story, Deschner told us, was that God was in Christ, and so it would be as though God had beaten himself in order to save us, not that Jesus protected us from God.

It wasn't until I had been in the parish ministry several years that I understood how important that understanding was for me and for those to whom I ministered. Most of us, I found, were afraid of God, and if we took the crucifixion seriously, grateful to Jesus for saving us from "the wrath that is to come," as John Wesley put it.

What a relief it was to be able to put that story and that assurance into place, and to discover for myself that we had it backwards: it was not *God* that Jesus paid with his blood. All these years I had feared God, wondering, "If God would ask such a thing of his own son, what would be asked of me?" It is a very different feeling to know that God came *in carne* (in the flesh) like a parent rushing into a burning building, to rescue us!

I hope that I have managed to communicate this fearless joy, this amazing hope, in these sermons, and that they may help others to let go of the fear and accept the wonderful love of God.

The Peace Treaty

In our nation, we are proud to say that nobody has any right to tell us what to do. No foreign power is superior to us; no outside body dares criticize us. We will take under advisement comments from our allies, but as *the* world superpower, we are the ones who will advise others, not the other way around.

This is also true in our personal lives. One of our chief values is self-reliance, the ability to take care of ourselves rather than asking for help. No matter what mistakes we may make, no matter how chaotic our lives may be, no matter how tense we are, "nobody tells us how to live."

Not even God.

Sometimes, it seems we would rather be wretched, stressed out, self-centered, even mean, than turn over our lives, our political decisions, our spending habits, our recreational activities, or our relationships to God's guidance. What we don't recognize is that in saying so, we establish a hostile relationship with our maker.

It is this state of affairs that Paul is pointing to in this passage. He tells us that he and the other apostles are "ambassadors for Christ, since God is making his appeal through

[them].'' They are like ambassadors opening negotiations between hostile nations.

The way Paul states the message from God is nothing short of astonishing: ''We *entreat* you ... be reconciled to God ... We are putting no obstacle in anyone's way.''

Christ entreats us? *God* begs *us*?

It is as though the President of the United States were to call you into the Oval Office and say, ''I am appointing you as Ambassador to North Korea, and I have a difficult mission for you there. I want you to beg for peace. What we want here is to overcome the years of animosity and suspicion. So make no demands, no threats; issue no ultimatums. Do whatever you have to do to get that message across. Whatever violence you may face, whatever their attitudes are, I want you to be conciliatory. Probably you will be followed and harassed; you may even be jailed — we can't know how this will go. Make no effort to find bugs in the embassy, put no scramblers on the line; everything should be completely open and above board. You understand? At *any and all costs*, we want peace.''

How would you respond? An ambassadorship is a sign of trust, and such an appointment is one of the highest honors any country can bestow upon a citizen. Yet here is the President of the United States saying that your safety as ambassador cannot be guaranteed — that in fact we can count on a hostile reception. You will be ambassador of the most powerful nation on earth, yet you are asked to go, hat in hand, to our sworn enemy and petition for reconciliation! Is this any way for a superpower to act?

But this is exactly what Paul claims: that he comes as an ambassador, carrying a petition for peace from the Creator, Sustainer and Ruler of the universe, to the creatures who are in rebellion against God's authority. I can say without hesitation that this is as ridiculous a situation as the idea of the President sending an ambassador to *beg* for peace with North Korea. In fact, *more* ridiculous, because we may actually have some cause to fear North Korea (they might have a nuclear bomb ready to use, for example), but God has no reason to fear us, no matter what we do, or what threats we could make.

So here is the unbelievable, prodigal nature of God: Hat in hand, God's ambassador approaches us, telling us that *God has surrendered*. Although our lives are nothing of what we had hoped and expected, lacking any great accomplishments to show for our time spent here, and although we have refused to take seriously the claim God has on our lives, God does not want to be our enemy, but our *friend*! God does not despise us; God *loves* us. God does not enforce our separation; God wants us to be at one with him.

To accomplish this, God sends as ambassador this travelling evangelist, carrying a new treaty — simpler than the first one, with all its codicils and *quid pro quo's* — to effect peace between God and us.

Can we see the Ancient One, sitting sadly on the celestial throne, waiting for our reply? Watching through the night, waiting for word from the long-overdue ambassador, who may be a new victim, dead at our hands, our hands that push away the very ones we love and need most in our darkest hours?

God is waiting for an answer to a simple message addressed to you and me: "Please be reconciled to God." "Please accept this gift I offer you, a gift of life, an end to war. A gift of love, obstacle-free, with nothing to hinder or trip the one who runs forward to accept freedom and peace." Nothing to make us wait. Insisting, in fact, that we *must not* wait.

"*Now*," the ambassador says. "*Now* is the time. There is no DO NOT OPEN UNTIL EASTER tag on this gift. Please open it. Open it *now*! I want you to have it *now*! Don't wait for 40 days. I don't need to wait until your house is in order. I don't want to wait until you think you've 'got it.' I am willing to suffer anything, any hardship. I will do anything to make you understand that you are loved, cared for, *wanted*. In fact, I already have. I have endured prison, beatings, riots, sleepless nights, hunger. I have done this because my Master asked me to, because it is so important to God that you hear this plea."

How shall we answer this petition of peace? How does *your* heart answer in this moment? Can we trust this offer? Or is it too much to hope for? Do you wish to carefully read the fine print?

Oh, yes, there is some fine print; this treaty is not cheap or easy. It is a tough treaty, paid for in blood. We have reason to hesitate, to consider the cost, to look inside ourselves. In a world with so little hope, we may find it hard to believe.

And still the ambassador stands at the door and waits for our reply. Will you accept the hope offered, the peace being held out? Or will you shake your head and walk away, certain that it is too good to be true?

What will you answer? The creator of the universe waits for a reply.

To Ransom The Prisoners Of War

Although there are several ways of looking at the Atonement, and equal justification for each interpretation, let us consider just one today: the idea that Jesus came as a *ransom for many* (Matthew 20:28). It is the basis for the statement Paul wants to make in this passage.

On Ash Wednesday, we considered Paul's claim that he had been sent as an ambassador on behalf of Christ, begging us to be reconciled to God, as though we were citizens of a nation hostile to God. This passage reminds us of another aspect of hostilities between nations — prisoners of war, held in dark cells or tiger cages, chained, often mistreated, waiting for some sign of hope, of deliverance.

It is difficult in the extreme for us to admit that we are imprisoned. We like to believe that we are free! It is the cornerstone of the American dream, the quality that draws immigrants from all over the globe. Our common credo is: "I'm as good as the next guy!"

But God replies, "You certainly are; you are as sinful as everyone else; you have failed to exceed the norm, and as a result, you are doomed to die, because the wages of sin is death" (Romans 3:23 and 6:23). If I am only as good as the next person, I am clearly in trouble! After all, how often do we say (in a tone that indicates we have given up expecting good), "Well, you know how people are!" as though we were not to be included in that category? Really, most of us share the secret understanding that if people knew what we were *really like*, they wouldn't like us (an understanding, by the way, that causes us to expend enormous amounts of energy covering up how we feel, what we think, and the secret sins we hope no one knows about).

Paul reminds us that the deterioration of the relationship between God and us started right at the beginning of the human experience. Adam (Hebrew for "humankind") was "taken prisoner" by sin. So sin was introduced by one man, but as in any epidemic, it spread; everyone has sinned.

Like Paul, the most honest among us acknowledges that "I do not understand my own actions. For I do not do what I want, but I do the very thing I hate .... I can *will* what is right, but I cannot *do* it. For I do not do the good I want, but the evil I do not want is what I do" (Romans 7:15, 18-19). In short, we are prisoners of war, taken captive by our own self-centeredness, our own narrow vision, our limited horizons. We are prisoners of sin.

If you don't believe it, let's look at ourselves more closely. When you hear of some horrible crime, do you want to go hunt down the perpetrator and do to him what he has done to others? On the freeway, do you become incensed when someone cuts you off, or makes rude hand signals in your direction? Do you ever say, "Give in! I can't give in on this issue! It's too much to ask!" Do you return angry word for angry word, lie when it's not convenient to tell the truth, hit back for fear of looking weak? Do you excuse yourself by saying, "It's a dog-eat-dog world out there, you have to look out for number one?" Sounds like we're back to "I'm as good as the next person!"

And so we are confronted by a piece of truth: We do not consistently *act* in the way a child of God would act; we usually *react* to what others are doing, often behaving in the very way we say we despise. Even worse, we insist on protecting our pride even when we know we've been wrong, because an apology will embarrass us. In short, we act just like the enemies of God, the very people we condemn.

Into the midst of this strides the Ambassador of God, bearing good news: We are to be set free, released from chains and darkness, self-loathing and fear. A prisoner exchange has been arranged, and we are all to be traded for one man.

In times of war, there are occasionally these exchanges of prisoners. But usually, some particular prisoner has exceptional value to his own side, and so his government is quite willing to negotiate for the release of many individuals in order to have this one person returned unharmed. In this case, however, the One who holds all the power not only has sent a message of peace, but offers a valued prisoner in exchange for our freedom. He will allow the Anointed One of God, the one who has never experienced separation from God, to be separated, to enter into prison in our place, so that we can once again be *at one* with God. We are not bound to continue in the hopeless, obsessive patterns that have imprisoned us. We will be free to be all that God originally had in mind for us. The original pattern will be restored.

What a message of hope! Can we believe it? Is it possible that we are that loved, that valued, that anyone would, of his own free will, enter into such an agreement on our behalf? We cannot clearly see what is happening here, but we can claim it for ourselves, even now, this minute.

Like prisoners in the darkest dungeons, robbed of even the simple touch of a human hand stretched out in kindness, we may be blinded by the light of the sun, but we may even now walk out into that brilliance.

We are truly free.

Unconditional Love

Have you ever stood at the side of a baby's crib, just watching the little chest go up and down, the tiny fingers curl and twitch just a bit, the tiny mouth make sucking movements? At such times, the heart just melts, doesn't it? We cannot help but love this little bundle.

What has that baby done to deserve such love, such an upwelling of protective feelings? Nothing, really — it just was lucky enough to be born *your* baby! Maybe just an hour ago, you were struggling to get some cereal in her mouth, between screams and tears. Maybe your little guy is teething, and for two weeks getting to sleep has been harder than anything except *staying* asleep.

Irritated as we may be, though, usually we clean up the mess, strip off the oatmeal-covered shirt, wash the baby, put some painkiller on those budding teeth, and try to comfort our little one until sleep sets in! Our love for our babies may wear thin at times, but love is incredibly elastic.

Some of us may have been disappointed in our children from time to time. Not every child who is well-loved, cared for, cuddled and powdered, turns out to be a successful, productive adult. Some grow up to commit crimes, turn to drugs, go from one job to another or one marriage to another, unable to find their calling or even a sense of stability in their lives. You may have had to learn to turn a child loose, distrust what he says, even protect your property or person from your child, but she will never stop being your child. Even if you have "disowned" them, out of anger or fear, they never stop being your children, as your midnight tears will witness.

This is the understanding Paul is leaning on in our reading for today when he says, "For the promise that he would inherit the world did not come to Abraham or to his descendants through the law, but through the righteousness of faith. But to one who without works trusts him who justifies the ungodly, such faith is reckoned as righteousness." Notice that Paul *includes the ungodly* in this — in other words, even those who *cannot measure up* to the stature of Abraham will receive their inheritance by *trusting* God.

It is certainly not that Abraham led an exemplary life himself, for that matter. This man lied twice to powerful rulers in order to save his neck; used a surrogate when his wife didn't conceive; at his wife's insistence, banished this hapless slave along with their son, in a desert place; and complained consistently about his lack of offspring, even though God repeated his promise as well as his care for Abraham numerous times. So it isn't that Abraham is an example of a perfect person, nor has he perfect trust in God. He is a person much like you and me — failed and imperfect.

Yet this is the man God decided to choose. This is the one through whom all the world will eventually return to God! And to this man, who has really done nothing to earn God's approval, God has made a promise. A treaty (covenant) has been made between the Sovereign of the Universe and this old, fussy, fearful man. And that treaty is good, not just for Abraham and his son and his son's son, it is good for *all the generations* who will trace their spiritual as well as physical ancestry back to him. And, Paul, speaking as the Ambassador of that Great Sovereign, says that this is an irrevocable treaty!

This treaty is not based on anything we may do. We do not earn it, Paul says. It is not something we can buy, like an economic treaty. It is not ever going to be broken by God, as treaties between nations so often are. It is not going to have a time limit on it, like the treaty that will soon run out granting Hong Kong the right to be separate from Mainland China.

This treaty is not based on obedience to any law, either. Paul says that our ability or inability to keep the law is not a factor! This is liable to be quite a shock to most of us, who are used to being loved conditionally — depending on our grades, how much money we have, what car we drive. We cannot believe that this inheritance is so certain!

But there it is, "For this reason it depends on faith, in order that the promise may rest on grace and be guaranteed to all his descendants . . . ." Guaranteed! An inheritance that is ours for the taking.

This, by the way, is the function of faith in our relationship to God. What good does it do to have an inheritance, if you don't believe it will be there when you reach for it? You'd continue to live in poverty, because you would never go to the bank to draw out the money!

So it comes down to this: A petition for peace has arrived. All those of us who are willing to call Abraham our spiritual ancestor, and to trust God when God says we do not need to be afraid, are granted a peaceful, happy, love-filled life on this planet, and in the world to come, life eternal. Do you believe it? If you do, reach for it.

If you still find this hard to believe, reach for it anyway. What would it cost you if nothing came of it? A momentary foolish feeling?

And if something does come of it, what a marvelous life awaits you! The quality of the rest of your life on earth depends on your answer.

Lent 3
Romans 5:1-11

The Hope Of Peace

Today's epistle lesson shows us Paul's legal training. Throughout his letters to the early Christians, Paul uses the language of the court system to talk about our relationship to God, from seeing Jesus acting as our attorney to this statement — that we have been *justified*: that is, acquitted or pronounced innocent. It is not the same word as "virtuous" nor "innocent as a child." It means that, having been put on trial, we are acquitted; we are free to leave the courtroom and return home.

The courtroom drama is a familiar one to those of us who watch television. A favorite ploy of Perry Mason-style mysteries is to have the attorney stand up in the courtroom and begin to peel away the layers of the crime, discarding theories and alibis one by one, turning false testimonies into a defense of the accused, so that the client — who is of course falsely accused — is vindicated in the presence of many witnesses. Unfortunately, this is not usually the case in real life.

I have seen a small boy, about four or five, standing in front of his father who was not a bit happy with his child. He had disobeyed his mother, left the yard, crossed a street to a friend's yard, and disappeared from sight. His mother, who had assumed he was safe in the backyard playing with friends, was frightened when she realized he was not where he was supposed to be. She had dropped everything, run into the street, and begun calling his name. When he didn't answer, she became distraught, and went to search for him. When she found him, she was not too gentle with him. He was an already-chastised little person when Dad came home.

Picture him: lower lip trembling, tears welling in his eyes as he faces his father. Now, he knows his daddy loves him. Daddy takes him for walks, and helps with his bath, and reads to him a lot of nights. Daddy works hard to see to it that there is a roof over his head, food on the table, and a lot of fun and games on weekends. In fact, that's part of the reason this tyke is so upset! He has made this loving daddy of his very upset. And Dad isn't yelling at him; he's saying, "Son, I'm very disappointed in you. You made your mother very scared when you disobeyed her. She was afraid you'd gotten hurt, or that someone had stolen you, or that you were lost and couldn't find your way home. She loves you very much, and does a lot for us. Didn't she make brownies just last night, because you told her you were hungry for brownies?" The little boy just nods, sadder than you can imagine.

Or maybe you can imagine. Maybe you've been in that spot with your own father or mother, being told how disappointed they were with you. Personally, I think that being told my parents were disappointed made me feel worse than when someone just stomps up to me and tells me how stupid I am, or how incompetent I am, or whatever. To be told by someone you really want to please that you have been *disappointing* is somehow much worse than the vilest epithet of someone less important in our lives.

Now you know this little boy hadn't started out to do anything bad. He had been playing with his friends, and when they all decided to go over to another little boy's yard to continue their play, they just ran off, and he, not wanting to be left behind, ran off with them! He didn't think about it. He didn't plan it. He just did it. And now here he stands, spanked by his mother and waiting judgment from his father. And he knows he disobeyed. But he doesn't know how he could have handled things any differently! How else could he have run with his crowd of friends? He just doesn't know how to explain it, to explain how he went wrong, and why. He feels terrible! And he's afraid.

This is about where we stand with God. We have disobeyed, and yet we have a good deal of company in our disobedience. We have wandered off the path God has directed us to, though we never noticed when we began to stray, and we have no idea how to get back to where we need to be.

Enter the attorney. We sit mutely, as the judge reviews our case, afraid that anything we say can and will be used against us. And then, to our amazement, the judge smiles and says our case is dismissed, that he understands why we behaved as we did. We are acquitted! We need not go back to the relentless self-questioning, the sense of failure, the fear and confusion. We will leave this courtroom by another door, a door that leads to closer fellowship with God and others.

It does not make our present life perfect. At this point, we have only "the *hope* of sharing the glory of God." It is a thing in the future, not a state we live in all the time. Right now, we can see the gleam of that day when we will be freed from all uncertainty and doubt; but we do not have perfect understanding, just because we are justified. We do not see face-to-face yet. We still see "as in a [brass] mirror, dimly." But we now have hope.

We have hope in another way, too: we have a new perspective on life. We no longer see the events of our lives as isolated, draining, depressing events to get through somehow, and we need no longer wonder why all these things are happening to us. Instead, we have some sense of the love of God in operation in our lives. We see how these disparate events can be made to work together for our good. We now understand that everything that happens to us, by plan or by accident, can build our character, if only we will give God control.

One day, that same little boy that we talked about earlier was out with some friends, and one of the guys had some beer. They weren't old enough to drink, and they knew they shouldn't drink in the car, but one of the guys pulled out a can, opened it and started to pass it around. That boy remembered in his heart that incident with his parents so many years earlier. He dreaded disappointing them. He didn't want to have to explain how he wound up in a car wreck because he was "just going along with his friends." So he asked the driver to pull into a gas station and called his dad to come and get him. His friends were pretty unhappy, afraid he would tell on them, and harassed him some. But when they saw his dad's car pulling in, they drove away. He told his father why he had called, and that he didn't want to be in that situation. They talked about being true to yourself, and being loyal to your friends.

Many years later, when that boy, now middle-aged, was faced with the possibility of making a huge profit in a slightly shady deal, he was glad for that earlier suffering. It had produced in him a strength to resist the easy-money temptation, and the endurance to work it through. He knew he had a loving God to help him build his weakness into a character that would endure.

It was not innocence that made him honest. It was working through the temptations, and having to live with the consequences of his actions, that developed his character. We all have our temptations. But we also have good news: God will always provide a way out of temptation and comfort in the worst of times. We live in the hope of people who, though weak, have been declared innocent, partners with God in a covenant that cannot be broken.

Lent 4
Ephesians 5:8-14

Come To The Light

Have you ever had the experience of losing all the electric power in your home? A friend of mine, who has a cabin on a woodland lake, told me that the worst part of the experience was that he kept flipping on switches as he went from room to room. He was so used to being able to summon up illumination this way, his subconscious kept insisting that it ought to work. The result was that he became increasingly frustrated with fumbling in the dark. He finally gave up and went to bed, only to be awakened when every light in the house came back on at 3:00 in the morning!

This business of walking in the dark (before Christ) is a major theme we see all over the New Testament. It perhaps springs from the Messianic prophecies such as Isaiah 9:1-2, which Matthew quotes at the beginning of his gospel: "... the people who sat in darkness have seen a great light, and for those who sat in the region and shadow of death light has dawned." Zechariah, father of John the Baptist, echoes that prophecy in Luke 1:78-79: "By the tender mercy of our God, the dawn from on high will break upon us, to give light to those who sit in darkness and in the shadow of death." John's gospel, filled with references to Jesus as the Light of the

World, begins with a great hymn: "What has come into being in him was life, and the life was the light of all people. The light shines in the darkness, and the darkness did not overcome it." And in 3:19-20, John picks up the theme again: "And this is the judgment, that the light has come into the world, and people loved darkness rather than light because their deeds were evil. For all who do evil ... do not come to the light, so that their deeds may not be exposed."

We are told that as the realm of God breaks through into our lives, it does so in a burst of light! For example, in Luke's birth narrative, the angels appear to the shepherds wreathed in glorious light, and the way of the magi is marked in Matthew with the light of a star. Even after the Ascension, we are told that while "Peter, bound with two chains, was sleeping between two soldiers, ... suddenly an angel of the Lord appeared and a light shone in the cell. He tapped Peter on the side and woke him, saying, 'Get up quickly.' And the chains fell off his wrists" (Acts 12:6-7).

Prison cells in Peter's day were pitch dark. Without electricity, there was no easy way to light the dungeons in which men were kept, and no oil lamp would be put in the hands of a man who might be desperate to escape his prison cell. So most of prison time was lived in dank, underground cells, in a darkness so thick as to be nearly impossible to penetrate, no matter how one might strain to see. Such sensory deprivation often led to madness, so that even when a person was released, their imprisonment might persist in their minds.

Furthermore, first century city streets had no illumination either. To be out at night alone was a hazardous proposition, as dangerous as in our cities today, but also perilous because of unseen obstacles that might trip one. To travel without a light was to risk serious injury.

For these reasons, darkness was not an abstract idea to Paul's readers; it was a real threat. They knew the power of a single small lamp, if placed on a stand, to illuminate a circle of family or friends gathered after sunset. A traveler on a country road, running late and moving as swiftly as possible to reach the safety of an inn for the night, would breathe a sigh of relief when he saw the lamps in the windows, announcing that he had at last reached his destination.

Paul is reminding us of Jesus' instruction that *we* must be that sort of beacon: "In the same way, let your light shine before others, so that they may see your good works and give glory to your Father in heaven" (Matthew 5:16) and "Therefore consider whether the light in you is not darkness. If then your whole body is full of light . . . it will be as . . . a lamp . . . " (Luke 11:35-36).

Paul himself has experienced the spiritual truth that he is preaching. He had been an enemy of those who called themselves "Followers of the Way," when he was blinded by a brilliant light, and the voice of Jesus spoke to him (Acts 22:6-11). He was so overcome, he says he fell to the ground and "those who were with me took my hand and led me to Damascus." The effect of the light was so great, that even those with him saw it, though they did not hear the voice.

It is because of his own experience that Paul is so forceful in telling us that the Light of the World (Jesus) calls us to take over the role of *being Light* in our own world. Jesus' own promise is that, "Whoever follows me will never walk in darkness but will have the light of life." "Everyone who believes in me should not remain in the darkness . . . believe in the light, so that you may become children of light" (John 12:46 and 36).

Paul never knew Jesus in the flesh. Peter could talk about the stories Jesus told, could call on his personal experiences with Jesus in times of difficulty. We might expect Peter to be singing hymns in the darkness of a prison.

But Paul is like us. He never knew the man Jesus, never heard him preach, never saw him raise a friend from the dead nor heal a Gentile woman's daughter. Everything he learned about Jesus he learned after Jesus had certainly died and had apparently been resurrected. Like us, he had to struggle with doubt, had to work through his salvation "with fear and trembling." Paul, of all the apostles, is the only one who, like us, walks *only* "by faith, not by sight."

From this, we can take heart. Some may be certain, some may know the will of God easily, but Paul knew what it was to walk in darkness and uncertainty. He knew the darkness of his life before being blinded by the light. He knew what it was to be set free. And as one who had been set free, he offers us freedom also. He speaks as one "born out of time" to a flock of people dismissed as "out of the flock" — us Gentiles. He invites us in. On behalf of God, who wishes us to be reconciled, Paul invites us in the words of an ancient hymn:

Sleeper, awake!
Rise from the dead,
and Christ will shine on you.

Lent 5
Romans 8:6-11

Choosing Sides

Do you remember those old cartoons (especially Tom and Jerry) that showed the characters considering a plan of action, being counseled by a devil on one shoulder and an angel on the other? Sometimes the little conscience and the little demon would actually come to blows, vying for Jerry to behave selfishly or kindly, remember?

Those cartoons said, in effect, that our lives are a battleground, with the angels and the demons fighting it out, trying to get us to choose sides. Every choice we make is a victory for one side or the other. In some of the religions of Paul's day, this was taken very seriously, because there was the common belief that whichever side had more "soldiers" in the day of judgment would win. Thus, every moral choice had implications, not just for me, not just for today, but for the fate of the universe as well! One never knows who will win in the cosmic battle. My vote counts.

Well, times have changed, and even this device has gone by the wayside. Our society — even our theologians — no longer believe in "The Devil." As Walt Kelly said through Pogo, a long time ago, "We have met the enemy, and he is us!" No longer do we say, as Flip Wilson used to say, "The devil made me do it!" Not in seriousness, anyway.

This may all be for the good: maybe we have stopped blaming someone or something outside ourselves for the problems we get ourselves into. Maybe we have begun to admit that we are to blame, that it is our powerlessness over ourselves and our impulses that has led us to difficulty. This would be for the good, too, if we would then follow through with the obvious: that we need to repent, make amends for what we've done, and reform our attitudes so we don't make that same mistake, engage in that particular sin, again.

Unfortunately, human nature being what it is, it is equally likely that we will excuse our behavior on the grounds that "I can't help it; I was — _____ (fill in the blank: abandoned, abused, seduced, misled, drunk, addicted, sick, and so forth)." And then stop thinking, working, amending. "Obviously," we hint, "it's impossible for me to change; you'll just have to accept me as I am, warts and all!" Never dreaming that our "warts" look like volcanoes from the outside!

This is not what the scriptures tell us. And if we continue to insist that people cannot change (which, incidentally, leads to me excusing my behavior constantly, while insisting that you need to be executed for breaking the law, among other things), then we will never realize what power the resurrection offers us! It is precisely the power of the risen Christ that Paul claims is life-giving and life-changing, if we grab hold of it.

That power means nothing if we do not realize just how powerless we are in the face of evil. If we believe that we have merely failed, then we will blame ourselves or others, but, in the false belief that we can change ourselves, we will continue failing and feeling wretched, failing and beating ourselves, failing and wondering why we cannot seem to do better. Even Paul had this problem; in the previous chapter of Romans (7:14-25), he shares with us his own struggles against sin.

He complains about his inability to do the right thing, even when he knows what he should be doing. He says that he knows the right thing, the spiritual thing, but then watches appalled as his baser nature takes over. He is trying to warn us that as long as we struggle with ourselves, thinking that we must heal ourselves, pull ourselves up by our own bootstraps as the saying goes, we cannot help but despair!

From his own personal knowledge of that struggle, Paul reaches the conclusions presented to us here, which are:

> that we cannot, by any means, whatsoever, save ourselves;
> that the only hope we have is to let go of our own ideas and turn ourselves over to God;
> and that we allow the Holy Spirit to begin to re-form us, literally regenerate us, from the bottom up.

But there is no middle ground. There is no place where we can have both the rule of the Holy Spirit and rule ourselves. "Those *controlled* by the sinful nature cannot please God." It's like having cruise control for your life. You know how this works: we can either be on cruise control or drive the car ourselves. As soon as we touch either the accelerator or brake, the cruise control cuts out, and we're on our own again.

In the same way, Paul says, if we have the Holy Spirit, we are controlled by God. If we are controlled by God, life gets to be lots easier, because some decisions are pre-made. We don't have to think about whether to be faithful, loving, loyal, kind, trustworthy, joyful, patient or truthful. We don't have to think through the temptations that confront us. We have already decided to leave the paper clips at work, to buy our own pens, to avoid washroom gossip, to put in an honest day's work rather than watch the clock and goof off, to not nurse resentments, to not return angry words for angry words, to treat others as we would wish to be treated.

There is even more: God promises that we will be resurrected, just as Jesus was, by the Spirit living in us. This is not a "maybe, if I'm very good, and the good things I do outweigh the bad things," or an "I can amass enough points by going to church, reading my Bible and giving ten percent of my income, I'll get to heaven." It is an absolute, a promise, a verified given. And if that seems too easy, too good to be true, well, that's the gospel, just the same. Like the decisions that are pre-made for us if we are living in the Spirit, the judgment as to whether or not we will share heaven with God is also pre-made. It's all part of the package.

Paul verifies for us that this is definitely the way of peace. It is the treaty, if you will, between God and us. We will make God the ruler of our lives, and God will promise us resurrection and peace. This is not a guarantee that our lives will be perfect, smooth, untroubled. It is a guarantee that when our boat is tossed by raging waves, we will have the inner peace and trust in God to be able to sleep in the back of the boat with Jesus.

This treaty has been offered to us by God, long before we even knew that we were "at war," before we had any sense of our own lostness. But the choice of whether or not to accept it, that still belongs to us. Will you agree to this arrangement? Will you opt for peace and the certainty of life eternal? Or will you insist on doing it all your own way?

Paul, the Ambassador of the Great Sovereign, awaits your reply to his Master's offer.

Passion/Palm Sunday
Philippians 2:5-11

To Bow The Knee

On this Passion/Palm Sunday, we both celebrate the triumphal procession that was due to Jesus as the Christ, and look forward to his betrayal and death just a few days later. And so, this passage from Philippians is exactly right for our text this morning. In it, Paul is quoting an early Christian hymn, a hymn that triumphantly extols Jesus, not just for the amazing work he has done on our behalf, but also for the very essence of who he was and is.

It begins by stating a basic Christian belief, that Christ "was in the form of God." In order to understand this, we have to understand the Greek idea that all of reality exists on two levels: the basic, underlying reality of what is (*morphos*) and the exterior appearance of the thing (*schema*). For example, all apples are easily identified as apples, be they crab apples, Delicious apples, Macintoshes or Granny Smiths. Their character is "apple"; but their exteriors can be yellow, red, pink, green or striped. Even their flavors and textures are quite different from one another. But they are all apples.

Paul is saying the same thing about Jesus. Jesus may not look just like God, may not have the same outward appearance, but in his essence, Jesus was God. Even so, Jesus did not think he needed to clutch his status to himself, demanding glory and honor and the worship of heavenly beings. Rather than "exploiting" (NRSV) his situation and his privileges, he gave it all up for us. If we may put this in earthly terms, he went from riches and glory and privilege, a mansion in the best part of the suburbs, replete with servants to obey his every whim, to becoming a slave. Not only without honor and privilege, but one who must jump when his master says "jump," no matter how tired, hungry or ill he might feel.

These days, in these United States, there are a lot of people living with disappointment. People who went to college, assured by others that this was the way to attain status and a good job, find themselves without work in their field, and "overqualified" for more menial positions. There are men and women who have had good, high-paying jobs for nearly a quarter of a century who are having to be retrained for the jobs that are now available, and are discriminated against because, despite having all that experience, they are considered "too old" to hire. There are families who split because to do so will qualify the mother and children for welfare, while dad struggles to keep a roof over his own head. There are women and children who have exhausted every resource, and who now constitute the fastest growing segment of the impoverished and homeless. And when those things are happening, you and I and others like us tend to start looking over our shoulders, fearful of what the future may bring, because we know that a job at McDonald's will by no means continue the lifestyle we currently have, not to mention provide health care for our children and ourselves. It frightens us. It threatens our peace of mind.

Don't you wonder how Jesus could have done that? Given up his status to become a slave? But here it is: He emptied himself, taking the form of a slave, humbling himself to be obedient to the point of dying — even the death reserved for terrorists and street scum.

Notice, it does not say that God demanded his death. Indeed, in John 10:17-18, Jesus is quoted as saying, "For this reason the Father loves me, because I lay down my life in order to take it up again. No one takes it from me, but I lay it down of my own accord. I have power to lay it down, and I have power to take it up again. I have received this command from my Father." Jesus was not acting under compulsion. He was not satisfying some blood lust of an angry God. He came out of love for us, to lay down his life *of his own accord,* a ratification of the treaty God wishes to make with us. He came so we would know that we are loved more than words can say.

After all, words are easy. We have known people to say loving words while stabbing folks in the back. Men have been known to tell women they love them in order to gain sexual access to them. Parents have been known to tell their children, "This hurts me more than it hurts you," while beating them. We will say, "Love the sinner and hate the sin," and then formulate the worst punishments we can think of for those "sinners" we supposedly "love." We will insist we are not racists, and then condemn all African Americans as lazy, all Native Americans as irresponsible, and all Vietnamese Americans as overachievers. Words are easy.

When it comes right down to loving someone, nothing beats what Eliza proclaimed in *My Fair Lady* — "Show me!"

And so, Jesus came to show us. A free, in-home demonstration of what love can do. "Greater love has no one than this: that I lay down my life for my friends," Jesus says. And then he goes ahead and *does* it. He surrenders himself to the authorities, principalities and rulers, a sign of God's tremendous love for us.

Isn't that amazing? In Romans, Paul comments that a person might sacrifice himself for a good person — but for a bad person? For sinners? For me? What kind of love are we talking about here? This is the kind of love we hope families may have for each other: the mother who lays herself over her baby in a house fire they cannot escape; the father who throws himself into the lake to rescue his child from drowning; the brother who offers his own kidney for his sister. But we are all impressed when a stranger risks his life for someone else. There

37

is no instinct to account for this, only a great, encompassing love for others. The kind of love that comes only through the Holy Spirit.

As we watch the events of Holy Week unfold, we watch in amazement. Who would offer himself to such pain for us? Who would assure his disciples of the ultimate good of what was about to happen, when he already knew they would not be able to hang in there? Who would say in advance of his own torture, "Be of good cheer"? Who would have left his own comfortable home, filled with every beautiful thing, to come and die in a forsaken corner of Palestine?

In light of all this, it is not surprising that "at the name of Jesus, every knee should bend, in heaven and on earth and under the earth, and every tongue should confess that Jesus Christ is Lord, to the glory of God the Father." Amen.

Maundy Thursday
1 Corinthians 11:23-26

Signed, Sealed And Delivered

On this night, more than on any other night, we consider the meaning of the sacrament of Holy Communion. Tonight, we gather in the presence of the Lord, and we consider the last meal Jesus shared with his disciples in this life. And at this point in the epistle narratives, we share with Paul a basic link: We are all talking about an event we did not witness with our own eyes, but a tradition that has been handed on to us.

Paul, remember, was not one of the original disciples. While those twelve who are named in the gospels gathered around a table in an upper room, borrowed for the occasion, Paul was likewise sitting down to the paschal feast, but in another room, gathered with his family, perhaps — just as Jesus was sharing with those who had become his family.

The Passover feast is, above all other things, a family festival, held in the home, with as much of the extended family gathered as possible, from the oldest to the babies in arms. The Passover feast is the celebration of the beginnings of community, in which all the members of the household are to be treated as family, including the servants and even travellers in need of a place to stay for the night.

Passover is likewise a celebration of the covenant that binds the community. It is a commemoration of other, more ancient events, that marked the beginning of the understanding that the offspring of Jacob/Israel were especially chosen by God: the demand that they be free people, the confrontation of earthly political power and the miracles that led to them being set free, including the night of death during which God's angel passed over their houses (the ones marked with the blood of the paschal lamb) and destroyed the first-born of Egyptian houses.

Therefore, Passover is primarily a celebration of life. A celebration not only that the chosen ones have survived, but a celebration of the fact that God is for life, rather than death. A celebration of the oneness of life, handed down from generation to generation, symbolized in the gathering of the generations around that festive table. A celebration of the continuation not only of life, but traditions, traditions that help define who we are, where we came from, and where we are all going.

On all of these meanings, Paul and Jesus were always in agreement. Wherever Paul celebrated that Passover, he and Jesus sang mostly the same songs, ate the same bitter herbs, drank the five cups of wine, and had small children ask the same basic questions ("Why is this night special above all other nights?"). Both meals began with the same breaking of unleavened bread (to remind them that they had to leave Egypt with such speed that they could not wait for bread to rise) and the same prayers; but suddenly, at his table, Jesus broke the tradition. Instead of the bread of the passover, he renames the bread in his hand: "This is my body .... Do this in remembrance of me."

Wherever Paul celebrated, this bread was not the body of Christ. He had not encountered his Messiah as yet. Like many people today, he was blind to the presence of Jesus, and would scoff if told that God was in a man on this planet that night, feeding his flock, not just on bread, but on eternal truths.

On both of their tables, Paul's and Jesus', there stood a cup of wine that would not be drunk from throughout the meal. It was the Elijah cup, reserved for that great prophet of old. It was said that when Messiah came, Elijah would come before him to announce his coming. And so, that cup was not to be drunk from, for Elijah might join them and announce who he was by drinking from it. At Paul's Passover table, it remained untouched for another year.

At Jesus' table, however, the cup was taken up at the end of the meal. His time had come. The announcement was to be made. He took the cup, saying, "This cup is the new covenant in my blood. Do this as often as you drink it, in remembrance of me." As each disciple drank from it, each one of them became, in a way, Elijah, ready to step forth and announce that the Day of the Lord had come, that Messiah is present, that communion with God is not only possible, but available right now, right here, in this place, at this table, in this cup, in this bread. God is here. We have seen, and we know for certainty.

For Paul, and those at his table, there was another year of waiting to look forward to, a distant hope that Messiah might come to save the people from their enslavement to Rome. For the disciples, there was a night of terror, a day of horror, and a day of despair to follow the drinking from this cup. But what a glorious revelation at the end of all that suffering! Paul would be spared the despair of this weekend, but it was just another Passover to him and to those with whom he shared this meal.

For Judas, there was no cup. At some point in the evening, Jesus turned to him and said, "What you do, do quickly." And Judas left. He went to sell information to the authorities, information on where to find Jesus, how to take him prisoner. While the others were singing their hymns, Judas was feeling the clink of 30 pieces of silver in his palm. While the others were wending their way to bed or to the Mount of Olives with Jesus, Judas was leading the palace guards to arrest Jesus. While Jesus was sweating blood, knowing what was coming, Judas walked quickly through the cobbled streets, and Paul was asleep in his bed.

Only God can know the heart of a person. Only God knows what Paul dreamt that night. Only God knows the motives of Judas in his act of betrayal. Only God knows how acute was the pain of Jesus that night, waiting in the darkness as his disciples tried in vain to stay awake with him. Only God knows our hearts, as we sit here tonight, gathered around this table, ready to eat this bread, to drink this cup.

Only God knows, too, how to commune with us in the places where we hurt the most. But God does know what our pains are. God knows our secret sins. God knows our secret desires. God knows how much we want to be part of the heavenly hosts. God knows how and why we fail in our good intentions. God knows.

And God calls us, as God called Paul. Like Paul, we were not there that first communion night. Like Paul, we have been apostles born too late for that knowledge of Jesus. Like Paul, we walk by faith, rather than sight. And like Paul, we celebrate what has been passed on to us from those who have gone before. In this feast, we are made partakers of the new covenant. We, like those first apostles, are called to be Ambassadors of Hope, bringing good news to those who wait in darkness. This feast calls us, nourishes us, sends us forth. "For as often as [we] eat this bread and drink the cup, [we] proclaim the Lord's death until he comes." Come, Lord Jesus. Be with us. Feed us. Use us, that we may be your messengers to a world in desperate need.

Good Friday
Hebrews 10:16-25

The Opening To God

Today we gather to commemorate the pivotal point in the life of Jesus the Christ. It is not the end of his life, despite it being the day of his death. Neither is it the denial of death — Jesus' death is real, as is ours. It is the recognition that, in the events of this day, death has changed from the darkness of the grave to a doorway which opens from one life to another. We have this confidence because of the events which the writer of Hebrews draws to our attention.

If we were in Jesus' time, and had the good fortune to be able to visit the Temple in Jerusalem, we would be very impressed with the magnificence of the structure. And we would be edified by it, as well, for all of the Temple was designed to instruct the worshipper in the ways of God and the authority of God in human life.

The first thing we would learn from the Temple is that God is extremely holy, and that there is, therefore, a necessity for intermediaries between God and humans, and a necessity for us to purify ourselves as we come to God. As we approach the temple, we find that the outermost courtyard, inside the fortress wall and a shady, columned walkway, is as close as a Gentile may come to God. In this Court of the Gentiles, open to the sky above, we would see the great golden basin, symbolizing God's control over the forces of chaos, and the huge sacrificial altar, with the savor of burnt offerings hanging in the air. Here we would be able to watch those who sell the proper animals for the offerings, the money changers, and the vendors of souvenirs and aids to worship for people from all over the world to buy. It is this area of the temple Jesus "cleansed" at the beginning of this week, driving out all those who were selling in the area.

Inside a many-gated wall is another courtyard, this reserved for Jews alone. In private rooms here, women would be able to take a ritual bath after the monthly time of "uncleanness," offer thank offerings after childbirth, and present their first-born to be bought back from God. Here are gathered the teachers of the Law, where men may ask questions of the priests and rabbis, where Jesus at age 12 was found, impressing these leaders with his wisdom.

In the midst of the complex, Herod had built a 15-story building, enclosing the Holy Place, in which the incense altar and the great seven-branched candlestick were kept. This area was reserved to the priests, who were chosen by lot to make the offerings. It was in such a place that Zechariah, father of John the Baptist, was serving when the angel announced John's conception.

Inside this space was the Holy of Holies, separated from the Holy Place by velvet curtains hung on golden rings. In Solomon's temple, this was where the Ark of the Covenant had been kept, with the two tablets on which the original Ten Commandments were carved. Into this place came only the High Priest, and he came only once a year, after a long series of purifying rituals intended to make him worthy to enter. It was his job to make restitution to God for the accumulated sins of the people, a job not to be taken lightly, for in so doing he represented all humans before God, and God to all the people.

Imagine, now, that we are in Jerusalem on this day in 27 A.D. Outside the city, a small band of ragtag men and women gather at the foot of a cross, on which hangs the man they thought would be their Messiah, sent from God to set the Jews free from their Roman rulers. Inside the city, there is a great hubbub, for it is the Passover, and people have come to Jerusalem from as far away as Ethiopia, Macedonia and Persia to observe the holy day at the temple. It's about noon, and we've just decided it's time to buy something to eat from one of the vendors and seek shade in one of the colonnades.

As we settle down to eat our lunch, we notice that the sky is growing dark. An unseasonable rain, no doubt. But then the ground begins to tremble, and in alarm, we run out into the open courtyard, for fear of the roof falling on us. In the midst of the panic, we hear and see a very strange thing: the curtain that separated the Holy of Holies from the Holy Place tears in two, and the room is clearly visible to all! What on earth — or heaven, for that matter — can this mean?

The author of Hebrews says that this rending of the curtain over the Holy of Holies marked the moment in which the final barrier between humans and God was destroyed. God, who had come in human flesh, has perfected the communication between us. This opening of that sacred space was God's way of telling the world that we no longer need a priest to represent us before God. Remember the words of Jesus reported by John? "I do not promise that I will pray for you, for the Father himself loves you ...." The very inner sanctum, the place in which we may see the face of God, has been opened to us all! We can enter for ourselves. We need offer no sacrifices to assure us that we have the loving attention of God. Rather, the words of Jeremiah have come true: "I will remember their sins and their lawless deeds no more" and therefore, "there is no longer any need of an offering for sin."

We don't need to defer to anyone with "more authority" to talk to God. The temple curtain has been ripped; we each may step forward to ask of God whatever our hearts most desire. We do not need to be in a cathedral or a temple to talk to God; we can go to our own private space and speak simply to God.

There is no longer a need to purify ourselves before we dare to talk to God; we may approach God and apologize personally, confident that God will immediately forget our sins! Just as we can, with the touch of a button, erase entire files from a computer, God will completely erase our sins, never to be remembered again!

There is no longer a need to fear God's judgment. God has opened the Realm of Heaven to all who would enter. With Jesus as our Great High Priest, we have a person who understands our weaknesses and identifies with our struggles. A cease-fire has been declared. We are free from fear of God, for we see now, in God's willingness to be incarnated and suffer and die for us, how much we are loved.

This is why today is called, for all its horror, "*Good* Friday." It is "Good" for us, who were afraid of God, and are no longer. It is "Good" for God, who missed having us close. It is even "Good" for Jesus, whose willing sacrifice accomplished all this.

The curtain is torn; the barriers are down. Through God's willingness to suffer even the death on the cross, our trust is restored. This is why it is "Good" Friday.

Easter
Colossians 3:1-4

The Power Of God For Us

Years ago, in a cartoon strip named *Tumbleweeds*, the captain of the fort sent his trusted scout to find out what was up with the Indians in their area. The scout returned, announcing, "Captain, I have lived with the Indians, eaten their food, taken part in their ceremonies and listened to what they say." The captain replied, "What have you to say?" And the scout responded, "Get off our land."

When we truly learn how others live and feel, when we have eaten with them, slept with them and heard their stories, only then can we truly be said to understand them. Like that scout, when we truly understand others, we will begin to identify with them. This is the meaning of the Christ event, the incarnation of God, who willingly offers his life on our behalf.

All through Lent, we have been considering with Paul the situation that existed before Christ came into our world; our aloneness, our isolation, our fear of God, our lack of self-worth, our tendency to choose our own way rather than rely on God's way. We have been considering Paul's claim that he comes to us as an ambassador of Christ, offering a new covenant that will reconcile us to God. This covenant was sealed in the sacrifice of the cross, in which we see God identifying with us, even to the point of torture, injustice and death.

47

Now we have come to the triumphal moment, the moment in which Jesus is resurrected from the stone tomb, the moment in which we are lifted from darkness to the Realm of Glory, the moment in which we see at last that God has in fact come to us. It is not an apparent moment until we actually get to the tomb. That is, we cannot stop at Good Friday, as Judas did, or we will never hear the good news. We cannot even just stop at the tomb, as Peter and John did, or we will hear but not understand the good news. We cannot just stop at hearing the good news from others, or we will disbelieve and despise those who say it's so, as Paul did.

We must be like Mary Magdalene, who knew her own weaknesses, acknowledged her anguish, her need, and stayed in the garden, crying her heart out. It was *because* she was powerless, and acknowledged her need of Christ, that she was granted a glimpse of the risen Christ. It was *because* of her tears that she was granted such joy. It was *because* her loss was so great that she became the first witness of the risen Christ. And the oral history of the Church tells us that she never wavered, never hesitated to say what she had seen, despite the disbelief of others and their dismissal of what she said.

It was not immediately clear to anyone, even his closest friends, that Jesus' resurrection is also a promise of our own resurrection. The disciples hardly knew what to make of it. They had to compare stories, recall what Jesus had said to them when he was in the flesh, so they could eventually remember that he had promised that they would no longer be his students, but his friends. That he had promised them that they would need no intermediary, but could go to God themselves, using Jesus' name. That he had promised that where he was going they would eventually also go, to a place he would prepare for them.

Eventually, they realized that the good news was better than they had imagined possible. Not only does God love us, but God intends to raise us, even as he raised Jesus, so that we may live forever, brothers and sisters with one another and with Christ! Their joy became so great, that they could not help but tell others about it. Their joy even overcame their fear of the authorities, both Jewish and Roman, so that no threat to their personal safety, their homes, their property, even their families, could stop them from teaching what they had learned.

That joy gave them a new perspective on life. Once our fear of death and judgment is overcome, you see, everything falls into different patterns than before. This is true of people today, as well. Think of the stories you have heard about people who have had near death experiences, as an example. Once they experienced that which they had feared, once they discovered for themselves that what the Church has preached for 2,000 years was true, once they had experienced firsthand the love and acceptance of the Creator, they came back to this life with new priorities. The values of Christ — love of God; a charitable attitude toward one's neighbor; the enduring nature of honesty, forbearance and patience; a life lived not in seeking pleasure but in seeking to serve others — become their values. They say exactly what our scripture tells us today: "Since, then, we have been raised with Christ, [let us] set [our] hearts on things above."

If we see ourselves in this light, we will begin, as Paul did, to see ourselves as though we were foreign nationals, living away from our own home country, keeping our allegiance to the Kingdom of Heaven while enjoying our service in this nation. After all, no one expects an ambassador to abstain from enjoying the country in which he or she is posted. How well can I represent the United States, if I despise everything about the country in which I am serving?

So we are not expected to *despise* this life, this earth, this nation. But we *are* expected to keep our eyes on the difference that exists between us and the population around us. God is counting on us to represent the interests of Christ and to hold out to our host country the benefits of being in covenant with God. While we will enjoy the customs of our world — having parties, eating, drinking, dancing, singing, shopping, movies, television, games, jokes, celebrating community holidays and festivals — these things will not be the center of our lives. We will keep our eyes fixed on home, the realm to which we will one day soon return, where there will be crowds rejoicing at our arrival.

We have this assurance, because of what we celebrate today — our "free home demonstration" of the power of God over all that troubles us. The resurrection of Jesus of Nazareth proves that power. The love of Christ proves that this power is intended for us. Our acceptance of this gift will prove its power to transform our lives. Our lives will prove this truth to all who see us.

We will be light in the darkness, salt to the hungry, joy to the grieving. We will draw people to us by the simple witness of our way of life, the peace that resides within us. And we will glorify God, from whom the power comes for us to be new people, for the creation to be renewed, for life to have new meaning.

Thanks be to God!

Easter 2
1 Peter 1:3-9

Surviving The Present Trials

There is one question that pastors get asked more often than any other, especially at this time of year. Can you guess what it is?

"If God loves us so much, why does he allow suffering?"

Sometimes it's a personal question: "Why am I having to suffer so much?" or "Why is the person I love so much having to suffer like this?" Sometimes, after a disaster, it's more general: "Where was God when the volcano turned into a sludgeslide?" Or when the tornado hit the church, killing even the pastor's little girl, who was waiting for the musical signal to lead a procession into church. Or when the tidal wave hit Medan, Sumatra, killing 11,000. Enter your personal question in this list.

This is not a casual question. Often those who are asking ask out of deep personal pain, trying to align their faith that God does, indeed, love us, with some horrible accident, or worse, some deliberate act of mayhem, such as a rape or a murder, or a birth-defective baby or some horrible form of cancer occurring in some deeply faithful Christian. If God is good, and God is all-powerful, why does God let this happen?

51

There are, of course, a variety of answers to this question. Some are simplistic and ignore one end or the other of that equation of God being both all-powerful and all-loving. Or they side-step the question altogether, as in, "We don't know what God had in mind when He allowed your wife to be murdered, but it will all be made plain one day." God's power is made clear in these statements, but where is the Love that took on our flesh in a cow-feeder and died on a cross so that we might know how much we are loved?

Other statements assume that everything that happens, both good and evil, is God's will. For example, "God has something in mind for your daughter, allowing her to be crippled in an auto accident." Statements like this do not take seriously the reality of sin, which means that *we can do things God does not want us to do.* If we can defy God, misbehave at our own will, how can we hold God accountable for the evil we do?

It would be wonderful, of course, if children were never kidnapped, accidents never maimed or killed anyone, rape never occurred, weather never devastated, volcanoes never erupted. But if we are to ask God to interfere every time someone conceives an idea to do evil, what kind of a world would we have? The rapist might be stopped, killed at the command of God, but what would God do to me when I screamed for the blood of the killer? When vengeance is uppermost in my mind? Probably none of us would have survived to whatever ripe, old age we are right now!

Furthermore, we know that there are certain rules in place for the orderly operation of the universe. Gravity is not overcome when we choose to stand on a folding chair rather than a ladder to reach down the heavy meat platter from the top cabinet. The laws of thermodynamics are not suspended because I choose to carry a boiling kettle across the kitchen, rather than wait for it to cool. The physics of electricity do not change because your infant granddaughter has found a hairpin next to the open electric socket. If we are going to ask God to suspend the rules every time someone is in trouble, the universe becomes undependable. You would never know, from one second to the next, whether laying a knife on a counter meant it would stay there or float across the room! It must be that the world can be counted upon to continue to spin in its orbit, revolve once every 24 hours, and that such rules as "two bodies cannot occupy the same space at the same time without injury to one or both" will continue in effect.

For what can we turn to God, then? Can we ask for the evil to be turned aside? Surely. Sometimes, the evil is indeed turned aside. Sometimes, a dream suggests a new direction to take, a friend offers us a new perspective on a problem, a mysterious stranger intervenes, a voice tells us what action to take to avoid danger, or the doctor's skill is enough to remove the tumor or cure the disease. As we learn more about how our planet works, how prayer affects our bodies, how listening to God (meditation) can help us perceive the way God wants us to go, our lives can be fuller, richer, and more satisfying. Our active acceptance of the guidance of the Holy Spirit gives us a sense of peace that, as Jesus promised, transcends any earthly peace we have known.

We can turn to God for strength and comfort in times of trial. We can take our pain, our grief, our fear, our rage, and lay them all before the cross of Christ. We can talk to the one who knows what it's like to lose a friend, be betrayed by a comrade, be ridiculed in public, suffer horrendous pain and die. The richness of the Christian understanding is precisely that we do not have a God who does not understand, who has never lost a son, who has no idea of the meaning of human loneliness. God does understand. He's cried in the dark, too, while his well-meaning friends snoozed nearby.

Peter offers us another suggestion, as well. He says in our letter today that God has given us *hope* — hope that the trials and suffering and grief we face will be used to refine us as gold is refined. Not that God *wants* us to suffer, but our sufferings may be used to make us finer than we were, more refined, more gracious, more understanding of others.

Suffering can go either way. We have all known people who, having lost a child, become bitter, isolated, God-hating people. Others, having suffered the same loss, go out and start organizations to remove drunk drivers from the road, insist that seatbelts and airbags be standard equipment on all automobiles, provide support for parents who have lost children to SIDS, or work with children in some productive, happy way. Suffering does not guarantee nobility of spirit.

Peter is suggesting that since we know that heaven is waiting for us, guaranteed, although nothing in this life is guaranteed, we may rejoice, even in the time of trial. Since we know that the ultimate things are in safekeeping for us, we may also hope that when troubles come, God will help us to withstand them. God will clasp us closely, as a dear child, and comfort us as a mother comforts her sick child. If God has been able to put away the ultimate evil from us, then we may hope that the temporary evils that beset us will polish us like a gem.

For no gold may be wrought without going through fire hot enough to burn away the surrounding rock, leaving the gold molten in the bottom of the furnace. No gem can sparkle without going through untold pressure for millennia, only to have someone chip away at the surface of the stone, so that it can reflect back the light it receives. Chipping, sanding, intense heat, pounding, all are necessary to produce the finest jewelry.

This does not give us a final answer to the question of evil. But Peter, the ever-practical businessman, points us to a more profitable round of questions. A series of questions that reminds us of our ultimate hope, to give us strength to endure present trials.

A Ransom Paid

A few years back, an evangelist came to a modest-sized congregation for a 4-day weekend revival. On the closing night, the congregation formed a circle around the sanctuary and the evangelist turned to the person on her right and said, at a volume easily heard by all, "God loves you. Pass it on." The message was passed through about one-third of the circle when a lady turned to her neighbor and said, "Jesus loves you," rather than "God loves you." Her neighbor caught the error and passed on the original message: "God loves you. Pass it on." But two people later, a man again said to his neighbor, "Jesus loves you. Pass it on." And so the message continued back to the evangelist.

This visiting preacher had a point to make, however, so with an expression and demeanor of all seriousness, she said to the congregation, "You have made an error, and it is a common one, but one that needs to be corrected. We find it easy to say, 'Jesus loves you.' We learned that lesson early, in Sunday school, from well-meaning teachers, who understood that Jesus was easier for a child to grasp than the idea of God. But what Jesus came to teach us is that *God* loves us. If we have not learned that, we have not learned any of what Jesus taught."

The group was tensely quiet. The evangelist looked around the circle slowly, turned to the person on her right, and said, "God loves you. Pass it on." This time, the message made it most of the way around the circle before someone lapsed, and the recipient of the message immediately replied, "No, that's not right. *God* loves you. That's the message we're supposed to pass on." Everyone started to smile, but one young mother started to cry. When others turned to her in amazement and alarm, she said, "I never heard that before."

One of the reasons the Church has insisted down through the ages that we understand God as a Trinity of co-equal *personae* (Creator/Father, Redeemer/Son, Sanctifier/Holy Spirit) is that otherwise we will tend to see Jesus, who loves us, as coming to rescue us from the wrath of the Father, who judges us as despicable sinners. Indeed, many popular evangelists have tended to take this attitude, and some of the most powerful historical sermons tend to see us as "Sinners in the Hand of an Angry God,"[1] dangling perilously close to hell.

But if we look closely at what Peter is saying here, we will notice that Peter says "you were ransomed" from the attempt to be righteous by force of will or self-discipline according to rules and laws. "Ransomed . . . not with perishable things like silver or gold, but with the precious blood of Christ . . ."

Now, if a child is kidnapped, and a ransom demanded, who pays the ransom? Isn't the ransom demanded *from* the parents? And to whom is a ransom paid, but the kidnapper? And what price will a loving mother pay to redeem her baby? Would she not lay down her own life for the child of her own body? What devoted father would not go to the bank and pay every cent he had, if he had to, to redeem his child?

Peter says *we* are the children, kidnapped by the world, to be enthralled by computer games and bingo, entranced by television rather than relationship, more devoted to shopping than to caring for the poor, electing politicians as long as they don't raise *our* taxes, and voting them out if they seem to favor some other special interest group than ours.

It is as though we have been mesmerized by some fairy tale witch and are now trapped in the land of sugar plums. Every once in a while we may feel some pang of conscience, some momentary desire for something that goes beyond our world bounded by glitz and the latest fashions in everything from earrings to $40,000 cars. Every once in a while we may look around us and wonder, is this all there is? Just a round of getting whatever your heart desires, and then paying the bills and worrying what we'll do for money when retirement time comes?

Our release has not been easy. Like the hero in some tensely plotted suspense movie, Jesus has had to search for us. And we have been innocently bobbing along with all the other sheep, each of us wondering if we're the only ones who are aware of how life has declined in this country which once was great and is now sinking under the weight of the consumer society and the "feel good" morality we're fed from every direction. Like one of those monster movies, in which those who have had their brains sucked out keep assuring the rest of their community that "it's really okay; you'll like feeling this way once we re-program you," we have learned that we cannot be certain whom to trust by looking. We don't even know if we can trust the "professional" Christians.

In the end, Jesus was captured by the evil forces, the "powers and principalities" as Paul put it, and his life was taken from him. Tortured, executed publicly like a common traitor, buried in a borrowed tomb, he was exulted over in his death throes by those whose interests were met by the fear of the people. The one who came as ransom was dead. They had killed the one who claimed to speak for God, and figured that was that. The ransom was paid, but the captured were not set free. The reign of terror was still in place.

But God had a surprise waiting for them. The dead did not stay dead. The one who came to pay the ransom was himself raised from the dead. "Through him you have come to trust in God, who raised him from the dead and gave him glory, so that your faith and hope are set on God." Our faith and hope were given to us by Jesus the Christ, but he intended that our gratitude should go to God. The point of the sacrifice was to show us how much God loves us, not how much God demands of us, nor that God is bloodthirsty, and needed to have his appetite slaked. The point of the sacrifice was to show us just how far God was willing to go to bring us home — not just down to his last cent, but down to his willingness to suffer as we suffer, to die as we die.

What more could God do to tell us we are loved, wanted, cared for, of ultimate value? What an amazing gesture this is, that God should come in human flesh and suffer so for us!

"So what does God want?" the suspicious may ask. Well, it is true that God wants something in return. God wants us to be so overwhelmed by the grace shown to us that we will overflow with love for God, but also, that we will purify our souls by obedience to the truth so that we "have genuine mutual love," that we will "love one another deeply from the heart."

When partition came to India, and the Moslems and the Hindus were in civil war, Mahatma Gandhi fasted to bring an end to the turmoil. As he approached death, a Hindu rushed at him on his litter, and threw a crust of bread at the saint. "Eat!" he demanded. "I am going to hell, but I will not have your death added to my burden!" Gandhi, through parched lips, asked how he had earned hell. "I killed a Moslem child," he said. "I threw him against a wall, and broke his head, because a Moslem had killed my son."

"I know a way out of hell," Gandhi replied. As the stunned man listened, Gandhi told him, "Go and find an orphaned child, a Moslem orphan, and adopt him. Take him home to be your son, and raise him to adulthood. But be sure you raise him as a Moslem, in your home."

When we can learn such love for each other, we will have realized the ransom that has been paid for us, the children of God, bought back from death by the blood of Jesus, who was God, in the flesh. When we can demonstrate such love, we shall be set free from sin, and will know how much we have been worth to our loving Father.

———————————

1. A sermon of the late Jonathan Edwards.

Easter 4
1 Peter 2:19-25

Giving Better Than We Expect

The boss had called the receptionist into his office for one of those chats we all dread. He was displeased with her demeanor in the office. For the most part, she was efficient, did her work on time, and seldom put through a call incorrectly. But her attitude needed an adjustment, he said. He didn't like the way he heard her talking to some of their clients.

"Well," she replied, "I really don't have a bad attitude. I treat people pretty much the way they treat me. If they're pleasant, and easy to get along with, and polite, then I'm the same way to them. But we have some clients who are rude, abrupt and demanding, and I have no intention of changing the way I act toward them. If they want to be treated better, they'd better clean up their act."

The boss was floored. "But that's not the way I want it to be around here!" he exclaimed. "I want you to treat the customers well no matter how they treat you! I want you to treat them the way you want to be treated!"

Now it was the receptionist's turn to be floored. "Why should I?" she replied. "If they're rude to me, they don't deserve any better!"

Even in the secular world, there is an understanding that there are two ways to behave. We can be *reactive* — that is, we can react to how others treat us, what they say to us, and respond in kind. Or, we can be *proactive,* and set the tone for how the interaction will go. If we want to set a tone for our business, office or factory, we behave proactively — as we want to be treated, despite how others react. We compliment people whenever possible, maintain a positive atmosphere, and refuse to return anger for anger. We avoid sarcasm, listen carefully to one another's feelings, and try to help each other be all that we can be. Managers are paying people a lot of money these days to have employees learn how this sort of approach leads to a happier atmosphere and improves customer satisfaction, leading to a more successful business.

Isn't it funny that the people of the secular world can see the benefits of following what Jesus has taught us, whether they claim to follow him or not? How much more, then, should we Christians attempt to model ourselves the same way? As our scripture for today says, "For to this you have been called, because Christ also suffered for you, leaving you an example, so that you should follow in his steps . . . . When he was abused, he did not return abuse; when he suffered, he did not threaten; but he entrusted himself to the one who judges justly."

Of course, this way of life is not easy. It takes deep motivation to practice being this way. Unfortunately, the place that employs us generally has more clout to change people, by imposing sanctions (such as possibly losing our jobs) to induce us to conform. Now that I think about it, that's probably why some preachers fall into preaching about the horrors of hell every once in a while — to scare us into behaving!

We have a tendency, most of us, to justify our behavior. Children will usually say quickly, "Well, he started it!" But as we peel back the incident, we find that "he started it" by escalating name-calling or nit-picking or teasing into a hitting match. And the same name-caller may very well be the one who first protested innocence.

Unfortunately, although we grow taller, many of us never mature. We continue the "he started it" routine, though we may call it by different names. "He can't talk to me like that," the angry wife says, as she drives to the mall, credit card in purse, where she winds up overspending in an angry power binge. And many an alcoholic will tell you, while in the throes of drink, that "she drove me to it. She picks at me all the time, and I get enough trouble from my boss and the customers. I shouldn't have to take it at home, too." Or like Adam and Eve, we blame the snake.

It is not a common value in our society to take any seeming injustice calmly, especially when we're the ones suffering the injustice! We like to criticize those who threaten to sue anyone who seems to be abusing them, but none of us, it seems, is willing to take anything "lying down." The first reaction of many to violent crime these days seems to be to buy ourselves another gun. We are unwilling to trust God for our safety, and apparently are quite willing to kill anyone who "tries anything" with us.

What, then, do we do with Peter's comment that ". . . it is a credit to you if, being aware of God, you endure pain while suffering unjustly. If you endure when you are beaten for doing wrong, what credit is that? But if you endure when you do right and suffer for it, you have God's approval." In our society, isn't this a theology of "wimpiness"? Who would be so stupid or so wishy-washy as to suffer in silence? Who wouldn't speak up to say "Now wait a minute, guys, I'm innocent here. I demand an apology."

Peter's answer: "[Jesus] himself, [who] bore our sins in his body on the cross, so that, free from sins, we might live for righteousness; by his wounds you have been healed. For you were going astray like sheep, but now you have returned to the shepherd and guardian of your souls."

"No student is greater than his master," Jesus reminds us. How much better would we do if we took it upon ourselves to truly walk in our Master's steps? After all, he could have said, "Why should I take this for them? They deserve what they get!"

Working In The Family Business

How everyone loves a newborn baby! We cannot help but turn when we hear the distinctive cry of a very new person. And when we see new babies, we almost always go over for a look, even if we don't talk to the parents. It's instinctive, really — an inborn guarantee that this tiny infant, dependent for its every need on the goodwill of those around it, will get what it needs. So when the baby cries, mothers who are nursing find that their bodies automatically "let down" the milk, and even if they wanted not to listen to their babies, they must, or suffer severe pain. Baby needs that milk, because it cannot grow without it.

After all, babies are expected to grow up, and if we find this baby six months later, unable to hold its head up, not responding, not even moving away from the mewling sort of cry she had at birth, we begin to understand that something is wrong. And if a child gets to be 3 or 4 or 5, and still acts the same as when he was born, we know for certain that he will never be anything more than he is right now, and that is very, very sad. We hoped he would be able to take a place in our society, and he cannot.

The same may be said of Christians. Peter says that we are to grow up in our salvation. We are not, in other words, to take the attitude that "I'm saved; God's work is done." Unfortunately, we've all met Christians who go around constantly proclaiming their salvation, asking others if they've been saved, and then going merrily on their way, not understanding that there is more work to do here! We all need advice on how to go further in the Christian life, and we need people who will come back and say, "So, now that you're saved, how is your life progressing? What have you done for the Lord lately?" If someone asked you that question today, how would you respond?

Peter says that we are "like living stones, being built into a spiritual house," with Christ as the living cornerstone. We are to be a holy priesthood, offering spiritual sacrifices, just as Jesus, our high priest did and does. So let me ask you today: How are your studies for the priesthood coming along? Have you made any progress in the work that God has asked you to do?

Some of you look stunned! Didn't you know that your destiny was not simply to be "saved" so you could go to heaven? Didn't you know that God has work for you to do? Have you been doing nothing? Probably some of you are thinking, "I'm not called to be a pastor! That's a very special calling! Surely I would know if that's what God had in mind for me?"

Yes, being a pastor is a very special calling. Not everyone is called to this job. You have to have ability in public speaking, and counseling, and training in keeping records, and visiting the sick and shut-ins and, oh, you know. Lots and lots of meetings. No, not everyone is called to be a pastor.

But every Christian person is called to be a priest. Every Christian person is called to "offering spiritual sacrifices." That's an interesting phrase, don't you think? Not one we talk about much, and definitely one that needs some explanation.

If we belonged to certain Christian denominations, we would understand the phrase to mean we were on the lookout to offer the various pains of our lives to God as sacrifices on our part. A woman's husband winds up crippled, for example, and every time she puts medication on his bedsores, she offers up that chore to God, so that God can give meaning to her unpleasant chore, and her discomfort can be turned to spiritual benefit for her. Some people in these churches deliberately undertake unpleasant chores for the love of God: for example, doing laundry in a shelter for the homeless, or going along the highway or through parks picking up trash and debris, or doing chores around the church that no one seems to want to do. Many people have been able to endure enormous pain and accomplish great deeds by offering it up to God in this way, and we benefit from their spiritual sacrifices.

Some other denominations would look at this business of offering spiritual sacrifices as a call to leave our homes one or two evenings a week to volunteer our services to those in need. We might work at a shelter for battered women, tutor a borderline student, teach an adult to read, visit at the local jail, campaign for safer neighborhoods, serve dinner or wash dishes at a soup kitchen, write letters to obtain freedom for those imprisoned by tyrants. We might volunteer at a local school, library, zoo, museum, or other community institution, to provide services that otherwise would be too expensive to offer or to help the handicapped enjoy a visit to these places. On a more personal level, some people offer their help to the elderly or those living alone, helping them clean their rain gutters or wash the outside windows, shoveling snow or driving folks to the store or hospital, or just taking an occasional casserole to someone living alone. Others work with children or teens, being a Big Brother or Sister, or working in a neighborhood house or with the scouts or 4-H.

Most Christians would agree that spiritual sacrifices might be the intentional pursuit of traditional spiritual disciplines: carving time out of each day to pray extensively for people we have heard are in need of God's help (like your pastor, or a list of the sick or shut-ins, or praying over the morning news stories); doing regular in-depth Bible study rather than simply reading some passage before bed; getting up 15 minutes earlier than we used to so we can spend time with God in the silence before the tumult of the day begins. We might fast and pray rather than spending our lunch hour playing cards and chowing down junk food. We might give up some small thing we indulge ourselves with and give the money to second-mile giving. We might begin to tithe (give 10 percent of our income to charity) and look for places to trim our budget so that tithe can come right off the top of our check-writing. Or we might simplify our lives, choosing to have less variety in our wardrobes or meals, cutting down on the use of cosmetics or jewelry so that we can support a special ministry, or help a young person go to college or technical school.

This call for each of us to be a priest was one of the cornerstones of the Protestant Reformation. Those early reformers took it very seriously that every Christian is intended to be an *active* member of a congregation. Every Christian is intended to be on the lookout for those who have no one to talk to, who have physical problems that require assistance, who are hungry and homeless and hurting. Every Christian is intended to be dedicated to God, looking after God's business *right where he or she is.*

And if we take that seriously, we need to be about our Father's business, just as Jesus was even at age 12. We need to be preparing ourselves and studying, just as surely as any pastor or priest in the seminary. We are laborers, employed in the family business, taking pride in seeing to it that our Father's business is a success.

Accepting The Call

Last week, we talked about the call of God to be involved in the ministry of the Word to the world. Peter informed us that we are each called to be priests, offering up spiritual sacrifices. This week, as we continue to listen to Peter, we hear some advice or guidance on how to do that job. He says, "Always be ready to make your defense to anyone who demands from you an accounting for the hope that is in you; yet do it with gentleness and reverence."

We've all met people who want to give us advice, who just drive us right up the wall with the way they do it, haven't we? The fellow who stands there with this "know-it-all" look on his face, saying, "You know, I wouldn't do it that way, if I were you. You're going about it all wrong. Now, if you'd ask me, I'd do it differently." The woman who says, "You're not going to do it that way, are you? Here, let me show you how to do that!"

We've probably all met people who use religious language in the same way. They get this patronizing look on their faces and spout off enough Bible verses, some of them misquoted, too, to drive even a saint crazy! (Which we weren't, they were right about that — and even less so, now that we're getting

69

edgy over their approach.) One fellow told me he wanted a good, solid Bible course so he could quote right back at them; he wanted to say, "I'll see your 1 Peter 3:1 and raise you a Galatians 3:28!"

But this is not the way God intends for us to behave. We are to be as ambassadors of Christ to the world in which we live. And whom do we choose as ambassadors to represent our country in other nations? Do we choose those who thunder and pound desks with their shoes, swear or use other rough language, who are rudely blunt, or arrogant? Not usually! "The Ugly American" is a *persona non grata* in the Peace Corps or career foreign services. We want someone who will represent the best that America has to offer, not a person who will embarrass us.

This does not mean that we want ambassadors who will "give away the farm" either! Ambassadors need to be firm, need to be clear about where their government stands, and need to be able to state those stands and expectations in a way which will be understood without being rude, if possible. Words must sometimes be chosen very carefully to get the message across without precipitating war or the eviction of the ambassador from the host country.

In the same way, God doesn't intend for us to try to win people by haranguing them. A quiet word of witness, a statement of how our faith in Jesus affects our lives, will plant a seed that will grow up later to bear fruit in the life of that person. A harsh word, a judgmental word, a cruel word, may turn that person off and put a stumbling block between him and God. And we need to pay attention not just in times when we are aware we are witnessing, because we never know when what we say or do affects others, nor what the outcome will be.

There's a story told that a couple of recovered alcoholics were called to try to talk to a guy who had rented a room in a real dive and seemed intent on drinking himself to death then and there. They went to the place together as a sort of protection, climbed a staircase that was half in the dark, went down a hallway that reeked, and found this guy's room. They went

70

in, despite receiving no reply to their knock, and found the guy half passed out on the bed. They tried talking to him, telling him their own stories of recovery, but got no response. One of the fellows pulled out a pocket testament, and laid it on the table beside the bed. "I'm leaving this Bible for you," he said to the man, "because maybe you'll come to and read it in the morning. My number is on the inside cover. I'll come and see you whenever you call. I want you to know life doesn't have to be like this."

The next day, the hotel manager called to tell them that the fellow had died in the night, and to thank them for coming, even if it didn't do any good. A couple of months later, the man who had left the Bible got a phone call. The voice on the other end of the line said, "I want to thank you for what you did for me that night. I read a lot of that little Bible and went to A.A., and I've been sober for over a month now. I even have a job!"

"Wait a minute, buddy. I have no idea how you got my name and number, but the man I came to talk to died that same night. The hotel manager called and told me."

"Oh, I wasn't the man on the bed. I had fallen asleep and rolled *under* the bed, but I heard every word you said, and when you left, I took the Bible."

Apparently, the right words were spoken to a man ready to hear and act on them. When we are listening to God in our own lives, or as Peter puts it, "sanctifying Christ as Lord in our hearts . . . appealing to God for a good conscience," we have a quiet confidence that makes what we say carry more weight with others. People really can see a difference between the woman or man anchored in the Lord and those who are drifting aimlessly with the tide. And people tend to seek out those in whom they see that solidness, to seek advice and an example of what it is to live in the Lord.

Because it is always true that our example speaks far more loudly than any words we might "preach" at people. And no matter what we say, if we can't even run our own lives, no one will be interested in anything we have to say about theirs.

So we prepare ourselves. We prepare ourselves to hear the word of God for our own lives. We prepare ourselves to listen for the voice of God in our own affairs. We prepare ourselves to speak simply, gently, from our own experiences, not lording it over others, but speaking from our weaknesses as well as our strengths. We prepare ourselves to speak of the "hope that is in us." We prepare ourselves to speak out of the very depths of our own life's pains to the hearts of those who are still in bondage, waiting for someone to bring them a word of life. We prepare ourselves to be laughed at, or ridiculed, so that we will not be defensive. We prepare ourselves to put our hearts at the disposal of those in need. We prepare ourselves in every way to represent the love of God to a world desperately in need of that love. And we prepare ourselves for surprise after surprise, because there is no limit to what can be accomplished by a person so open to the movement of the spirit. For the Lord whom we represent is the one who, as Peter reminds us, has "angels, authorities, and powers made subject to him."

Ascension Of The Lord
Ephesians 1:15-23

"But Some Doubted"

It is interesting to note that in Matthew's account of the Ascension, he says, "Now the eleven disciples went up to Galilee, to the mountain to which Jesus had directed them. When they saw him, they worshipped him; *but some doubted.*" He gives absolutely no explanation for this either.

What did they doubt? Did they doubt that it was Jesus? Did they doubt that he had been dead, or that he was apparently alive before their eyes? Since they were doubting before Jesus apparently rose into the air and disappeared into a cloud, we can assume levitation was not the source of their doubt.

Theologian Rudolph Bultmann says that everything changed for the disciples when Jesus apparently rose from the dead. There were those who had seen him since the resurrection had been proclaimed, and those who had not. Those who had not, despite everything their friends and families told them, did not believe what they were being told. Those who had could not be dissuaded from telling everyone that Jesus had survived the grave and appeared to them. Thomas, you will recall, told the others that he would believe when he could touch with his own hands the wounds he had seen on Jesus' body; and Jesus granted him the favor of doing exactly that, with only a dry reprimand that Thomas was blessed because he at least accepted what his eyes had seen and his hands touched.

Thus, we talk about the post-resurrection faith and the pre-resurrection faith as being two very different ways of knowing Jesus the Christ. Those who never knew the Jesus who ate and drank and taught and laughed and walked and sweated have a very different sort of relationship with him than those who saw him angry, tired and hungry. The faith that the post-resurrection followers have was much more difficult for those who had known Jesus in life. They who had walked with him had a hard time shifting gears, apparently. And you can understand this. It's as though your sister had just been elected President of the United States, and now you have to remember to call her "Ms. President" rather than Sally.

We post-resurrectionists, on the other hand, come much more readily to Jesus as the son of God, the Anointed One, the worker of miracles, the one who is present in our lives every day, to whom we talk, from whom we beg favors, to whom we cry when things aren't going well. Since we have no dissonance from another, previous relationship with Jesus, we have the privilege of acceptance of his special nature. Assuming we have any revelation of God, our revelation is the one that comes from knowing the claim that Jesus rose from the dead, and knowing this before we know much else about him.

It is this sort of revelation that Paul also has known. He saw Jesus, not visually, but "with the eyes of the heart." His experience was mystical, but powerful, life-changing! He was never the same. He became absolutely certain of those things he disbelieved entirely just a moment before!

Paul prays that we, too, will have this experience. Not just so we might have a "religious experience," but so that we "may [now] know what is the hope to which he has called [us]," and "what are the riches of his glorious inheritance among the saints." In other words, the mystical experience is not just to contemplate, trance-like, the wonderfulness of Jesus. It is supposed to give us **hope**.

Notice the word *hope* — not certainty, necessarily, though some of us here today are *absolutely certain* that God loves us, that death of the body is not the end of the person, that there is a place prepared for us in the Reign of God, and that one day we will find ourselves in the place where we feel most at home, with that "god-shaped space in our hearts" (as Martin Luther said) filled to the brim with God.

But others of us here today are like those disciples on that hilltop. We have our doubts. We are not certain that death is but a doorway into another dimension. We fear meeting God because we are not certain that what Jesus did in dying for us comes anywhere near what we need in order to see God and live. We are not certain that we can by any means enter the "strait gate" as the old King James English put it. Our hope is a more tenuous thing, more fragile than we wish it to be.

Paul goes on to say that he wishes we could know "what is the immeasurable greatness of his power for us who believe, according to the working of his great power," the power that God put "to work in Christ when he raised him from the dead ... and [put him] above every name that is named, not only in this age but also in the age to come."

Note that word — **power**. If we knew the power of God, power so incredible that it could reanimate a body dead three days, power so wonderful that it drives out every fear and worry, power that gives a person the courage to die when he didn't have to, power that overcomes every obstacle that keeps us from loving one another as we have been loved, what would be left that we could not do? We aren't talking about mere muscle strength; we're talking the ability to heal, the power to forgive sins and have the recipient of those words be freed from what bound him or her. We're talking the power to make those bent under the load of life stand straight and tall; those paralyzed by uncertainty roll up their mats and walk; those bound by self-pity decide to get well.

That kind of power is very hard to come by. Some try to find it in a bottle, or sex, or fantasy games, or working 70 hours a week. Some try to find it in a gun, or by slapping others around, or constantly pushing at the limits of what others will tolerate. Some try to find it by acting crazy, and some try to find it by being perfect all the time. But none of those things work. And when we find they don't work, we end up either burnt-out, dead or in jail — or we just give up and decide to turn ourselves over to God.

Paul learned it the hard way. Some of us have to learn it the hard way. The easiest way to have that power is to give ourselves, our lives, our families and all we possess back to God, to whom they belonged to begin with, and to trust God for the results of all that we do. To admit that we are puny, powerless, trying to make order and succeeding only in sinking deeper into chaos. To recognize that in fact we don't even know our lives are chaotic and that they don't have to be.

This "spirit of wisdom and revelation," as Paul puts it, has indeed the power to put our lives aright, to lead us to a place where "the eyes of our hearts" will be opened. In that place, by that wisdom, we can begin to put our lives into the order God has in mind for us.

When we do that, the reign of God has actually begun for us, in our homes, in our minds and hearts. Others may doubt at first. But the results will be perfectly plain, as plain as the changes that took place in Paul's life, and that he wishes for our lives as well.

Developing Staying Power

Some people read this passage, and they decide that everything that happens to us is to be seen as a "blessing" from God. They will tell you, quite straightforwardly, that God has every event of your life planned, including anything that seems to be bad at the time. If that gives them faith that everything will come out right in the end, it could be a blessing. But too often, what happens is that we then think that every evil thing that happens is visited on us by God. And instead of being led to a renewed faith in the ultimate working of God, people become angry, and they turn away from God. Afraid to tell God that they're being treated unfairly, that they are angry at Him, they say nothing. They are hurt, frightened and isolated, even from the love of the One they need most surely.

But this is not what Peter is saying here. We need to read carefully to hear what Peter means to convey to us. Peter doesn't say that God wants us to suffer. He says that we suffer because we are of the house and lineage of the Christ. The suffering that sometimes comes upon those who are faithful to God comes precisely because we are cloaked with God's spirit.

A theologian of 1930s Germany was a man by the name of Karl Barth. Barth drew a word picture of our lives that portrayed us as living within the very periphery of God. All of the creation exists, he said, *inside* of God. Outside of God, there is literally *nothing*. To be outside of God is to descend into nonexistence. Satan has opted for this state of nonbeing, and furthermore wars against God. As Satan pokes at God, if that's where you are standing, you get poked. It's nothing personal; you have not been selected particularly; it's just that that's the point Satan jabbed at this time.

Now that may not be particularly comforting. But we need to understand that God does not choose to torment us or "test" us, despite what we may read in — or into — the book of Job. What Peter is saying is essentially what Barth says: We are tormented because we are seen as being God's people, and those who wish to oppose God will pick the faithful as targets for their wrath.

Some 30 years ago, when Rosa Parks refused to give up her seat on the bus to a white man, there was a general uprising in Birmingham. The African Americans organized and were trained for resistance to being evicted from their bus seats.

"What're you going to say, when some white man tells you to get out of your seat?"

"Excuse me, please, but I paid for this seat, and I'm going to sit in this seat."

"And what if they threaten to hit you?"

A little fainter voice: "Excuse me, sir, but I paid for this seat, and I'm going to sit in this seat."

"And if the bus driver gets up and tells you to get out of that seat?"

"I paid for this seat, sir, and I'm going to sit in this seat."

"And if they pick you up, and rough you up?"

Silence. Then, "I don't fight back, I just go limp."

"And if they throw you onto the sidewalk?"

"I probably won't be able to do much, sir! My bones will be broken!" Nervous laughter, then uproarious, all around.

They were standing up for what was right — the right to keep the seat they paid for, not to have to give it up to any person who told them to, just because their skin was dark. And they were beaten, and they were thrown to the sidewalk, and they were jailed. So they stopped riding the buses altogether, and started to walk to work and back.

Sometimes that meant getting up two hours earlier so they would be at work on time. But they did it. It usually meant they were getting home two hours later at night, too. Eating late. Shorter hours of sleep. But they kept it up. They kept it up for two years, until the wills of the bus company and the city were moved to allow each rider a seat, first come, first served, at the same price.

Do you think you would have that kind of staying power in the face of severe opposition, even violence? To walk to wherever you work every day for the next two years? How far would you have to walk? How long would it take? How certain would you be, after even a month, that "God will, after some small suffering, restore you and make you strong, firm and steadfast?" For what benefit do you think you would go through what those people went through?

And what if you knew there were some people who would not just rough you up, but put on sheets and come at night and drag you from your house and torture you and kill you? What if some of those people were the same folks who were supposed to enforce the laws during the day? What if you knew you had enemies who wanted you to die? How long do you think you could live that way?

Peter assures us that there is, indeed, an enemy in wait for us. "[T]he devil prowls around, looking for someone to devour [like a roaring lion]."

What is the crime for which we are hated? Being God's people. Having the name of Jesus in our hearts. Being clothed with the Holy Spirit. Trying to love one another as we have been loved. For these beliefs, these actions, this reality, we may be made fun of at work. If you are a teenager, you may be made fun of because you pause before eating to thank your creator for feeding you, or because you refuse to drink or use drugs or swear, or because you honor your parents. If you are a construction worker, you may be called a wimp because you refuse to harass women passing by the site. If you are a housewife, you may be made to feel inadequate because "all you do" is stay home to care for your children (and half the neighborhood, since "all you do is stay home").

What Peter is saying is, "Take heart. You're not the only one who was ever made fun of for being faithful to your spouse. You're not the only one ostracized because you work up to the quitting bell. You're not the only person who is shocked at what people do to each other. You're not the only one angered by co-workers who take home everything they need for a home office out of what the company supplies for use at work.

"But be careful. Your shock can turn to self-righteousness quite fast. We can easily begin to think we're better than everyone else. There are snares for all of us. So stay alert. Keep your self-discipline. But don't let anxiety take its toll on you. When you go to bed at night, don't fret. Give your cares to God, who knows better than we can imagine how to handle what's wrong here. Eventually, Christ himself will restore, support, strengthen, and establish you. Praise God, and in the end, you will have every reason to praise God."

Books In This Cycle A Series

Gospel Set

God In Flesh Made Manifest
Sermons For Advent, Christmas And Epiphany
Mark Radecke

Whispering The Lyrics
Sermons For Lent And Easter
Thomas Long

Christ Our Sure Foundation
Sermons For Pentecost (First Third)
Marc Kolden

Good News For The Hard Of Hearing
Sermons For Pentecost (Middle Third)
Roger G. Talbott

Invitations To The Light
Sermons For Pentecost (Last Third)
Phyllis Faaborg Wolkenhauer

First Lesson Set

Hope Beneath The Surface
Sermons For Advent, Christmas And Epiphany
Paul E. Robinson

Caught In The Acts
Sermons For Lent And Easter
Ed Whetstone

Tenders Of The Sacred Fire
Sermons For Pentecost (First Third)
Robert Cueni

What Do You Say To A Burning Bush?
Sermons For Pentecost (Middle Third)
Steven E. Burt

Veiled Glimpses Of God's Glory
Sermons For Pentecost (Last Third)
Robert S. Crilley

Second Lesson Set

Empowered By The Light
Sermons for Advent, Christmas And Epiphany
Richard A. Hasler

Ambassadors Of Hope
Sermons For Lent And Easter
Sandra Hefter Herrmann